You Can't Con GOD

Confessions of a Sinner

By Barbara Elizabeth Taylor

Edited by Jerry A. Stevens

You Can't Con God: Confessions of a Sinner
Published by Between U N Me Books
Copper Mountain, CO

Scripture taken from the New King James Version
© 1982 by Thomas Nelson, Inc.
Used by permission. All rights reserved.

ISBN: 978-0-578-39408-4
RELIGION / Christian Living / Personal Memoirs

Cover design by Natasha Brown. Interior design by Victoria Wolf, wolfdesignandmarketing.com. Copyrights owned by Barbara Elizabeth Taylor.

DISLCAIMER: This book is a memoir. It is the author's story and to the best of her knowledge the events shared in this book are as they occurred. The conversations in the book all come from the author's recollections, though they are not written to represent word-for-word transcripts. Rather, the author has retold them in a way that evokes the feeling and meaning what was said and, in all instances, the essence of the dialogue is accurate. The people in this book continue on their journeys and she is grateful for the moment their journey touched hers. If there are any mistakes, she does most humbly apologize.

QUANTITY PURCHASES: Schools, churches, companies, professional groups, clubs, and other organizations may qualify for special terms when ordering quantities of this title. For information, email between2@aol.com.

I dedicate this book to My Lord and Savior for His Mercy, Grace and Forgiveness and to my sister, Jeanine, and my nephews, Michael and Elliott, who suffered in so many ways as well. May they find peace, assurance, healing, and certainty for the future in Christ's Redeeming Love.

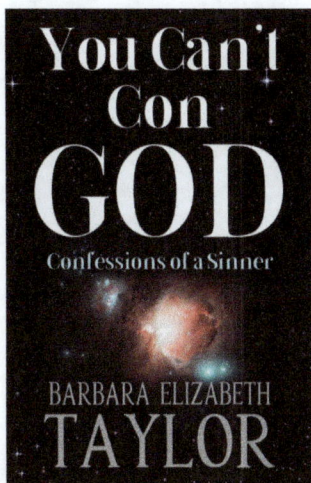

You Can't
Con
GOD
Confessions of a Sinner

BARBARA ELIZABETH
TAYLOR

Orion is where Jesus will return to take His redeemed Home for a thousand years. Afterwards He will bring the redeemed back to this earth with the New Jerusalem. The wicked will be raised and admit their neglect of not accepting Christ as their Savior. They will be destroyed as a match and Christ will create a whole new Heaven and Earth where the righteous will dwell for Eternity. They will have a Mansion in the City and another in the country. Every day they will learn something new and remember it for eternity as they travel to other galaxies, planets, and stars in the blink of an eye. Joy without end.

Acknowledgments

Internal pain is something no one can describe, as every individual has their very own feelings and experiences. It is impossible to tell someone, "I know what you are going through or how you are feeling."

I thank the Lord for giving me the courage to write my confession and for forgiving me, cleansing me, and assuring me of His Sacrifice that I might have eternal life.

My gratitude is extended to my editor, Jerry Stevens, and publishing advisor, Kirsten "Kiki" Ringer, for helping me to bring this book to press.

Thank you, Frank Fournier, for encouraging me to go forward in publishing my book.

I also want to thank my church family, who has loved me, encouraged me, and been there with me, throughout all the years. I ask their forgiveness as well.

You see, we are all so self -righteous in church, but when we leave church, that is the true test of our Characters. There are only two things we will take to Heaven – our Characters and those who have accepted Christ, as a result of our witness and the Holy Spirit's Conviction.

Prologue

Have you seen Barbara? I've been here for months now, and I haven't seen her. I know that there are millions of people up here in Heaven, but when I ask people if they have heard or met her, they say that they haven't seen her either. She certainly has to be here. I'm here because of her witness to me. Over the years she has been such an encouragement, support, and wonderful worker for the Lord.

I have heard many people share similar testimonies of always seeing a smile, a dedication to working for the Lord; her energetic, inspirational, motivational training all around the world, and her personal testimony that touched so many lives. Where could she possibly be? I've asked my personal angel to please take me to Gabriel to see if he might be able to tell me where I can find her, as I told her I wanted to live right next door to her when I got to Heaven. I'm sure he will be able to locate her for me.

And I saw thrones, and they sat upon them, and judgment was given unto them: and I saw the souls of them that were beheaded for the witness of Jesus, and for the word of God, and which had not worshipped the beast, neither his image, neither had received his mark upon their foreheads, or in their hands; and they lived and reigned with Christ a thousand years. (Revelation 20:4)

As we approached Gabriel, he was overseeing the Judgment Hall and stepped outside to visit with me. I reverently asked him to please help me locate a dear lady by the name of Barbara Taylor, as I had been looking for her unsuccessfully for quite a while.

He took me by the hand into the Judgment Hall. Slowly, he opened the books assigned to her name. "You see," he said sadly, "she isn't here. She confessed a thousand times to the Lord, but would not confess to those to whom she had not told the complete truth about her life. The Holy Spirit pleaded with her to not let her pride cover her sins, but she kept putting it off until it was too late. You see, you can't con God."

Since the day that Adam and Eve sinned, we all were born into a dysfunctional family. It just depends to what degree.

As I write this, I pray that the Lord takes away all my pride and self-sufficiency. I also pray that as you read this little book, you will not disclose any information that you might know about the locations I mention or the people's names. Please keep these things to yourself.

At the outset, permit me to say that I loved my father, mother, aunts, and other relatives in the only dysfunctional way that I knew how. When you grow up in dysfunction, you think it is normal. That is why so many abused women, as well as men, end up in dysfunctional relationships.

I was never taught healthy love from childhood through my adult life. I thought that if you said, "I love you" while making love to me, that that was what love was all about. In therapy, I only discovered later that while even animals may have sex for pleasure, that is not *love*.

For this reason, I think this explains why so many of us cannot fathom the *agape* love that God has for us. We have only been taught worldly love, or lust. That is why is it so important for us to focus on the true love of Jesus each and every day.

As a child, I wanted so desperately to be loved, and this carried over into my adult life as I experienced so many dysfunctional relationships.

Why did I wait so long to confess my sins? I still wanted to be loved. You see, only Jesus can offer me complete, unconditional love. I'm still working on that understanding.

Please forgive me for not being honest about my life, that is, until now.

Family History, Paternal Side

I close my eyes, thinking back on memories of my early childhood. My daddy would wake up my sister and me, bathe and dress us, and feed us oatmeal with raisins and cinnamon raisin toast with apple butter. It is a warm memory that I still carry with me to this day.

Daddy was tall, with dark curly hair and crystal blue eyes. Sitting snug in his arms, I always felt safe. I can't remember Mother ever holding me, but I'm sure that she must have when she was not working. Maybe it was just part of my life that I shut out.

Those early years with my daddy are the main memory I have of him. Unbeknownst to me, he came from a poor farmer's background and grew up in a very dysfunctional family which happened to be Adventist.

He was raised along with two sisters and a brother. He worked on the farm, possessing a ninth-grade education before dropping out of school.

It was said that Daddy had an illness as a small six-year-old child, causing him to sleep for hours under the kitchen table. His family never talked about it, for they were too proud to admit that he might have needed some medical attention.

As the second youngest, Daddy had been a nervous and frightened child, which carried over into his adult life. His mother was very rigid and strict, evidently thinking that she could earn her way to Heaven by being perfect without the help of the Holy Spirit. I'm sure that she did the best she could under the circumstances, but legalism was her dominant style.

Later in life, my father would work for a while and then find excuses for why things didn't work out and would go on looking for another job. After he married my mother, she financed a trucking company for him, which I was told came to about $250,000. He would haul freight, cattle, and other things from Indiana to somewhere up in Chicago.

I vividly remember that early one morning around two or three, Daddy got me out of bed and placed me in the back of the truck's cab, where I slept while he drove to Chicago.

At a truck stop, all the truck drivers, of course, made over me and bought me sugar doughnuts and chocolate milk. After all that attention, I became wide awake, like all children high on sugar.

I cherished that memory and always told everyone that when I grew up, I wanted to be a truck driver. I still have a great place in my heart for truck drivers, especially for those who make long hauls.

I later found out that my father's business partner in the trucking company embezzled money from the company. It eventually went bankrupt.

Over time, I only remember seeing my father when he would

occasionally come to my mother's or my aunts' to get some money or help.

My two aunts were very protective of Daddy, and most of the time he would either live with them or they would put him in a boarding house close to where they could help him. I'm sure they helped him financially most of his life.

Sadly, he was in and out of hospitals due to all kinds of illnesses, depression, nervous breakdowns, or coming back to spend some time with my mother. Why she ever took him in, I can't remember, but it was always a disaster just waiting to happen.

He would haul firewood in the winter months and do landscaping in the summer. He did beautiful work as a landscaper and was always in demand during the summer. He was expert at how to make the most beautiful lawns and landscapes around people's homes. Had he had the ability to run a business, I'm sure he could have been very successful.

When I would go into the drugstore, I would see him at the counter having an Alka-Seltzer, the effervescent antacid and pain reliever developed by some doctor from Indiana.[1] As far as I recall, and according to my aunts, my father took one every day.

Later in life, Daddy went down to Oklahoma to live with his parents until my grandfather died. My aunts took my grandmother up to live with them in Amherst, a suburb of Buffalo, New York, where the younger aunt was associate dean of the School of Nursing, at the University of New York in Buffalo.

For a while, Daddy lived at my grandparents' home before

---

1   *Editor's note:* Alka-Seltzer was developed by head chemist Maurice Treneer of Dr. Miles Medicine Company, Elkhart, Indiana.

moving into a nursing home in Stilwell, Oklahoma. Dr. Green, a very kind man, let him live in his nursing home in exchange for doing the landscaping around the facility and his own home.

Regrettably, my father later contracted Parkinson's disease. I don't recall seeing him after I started high school. Later in my twenties, though, I flew down to Tulsa to meet him before he checked himself into the state hospital, as he knew that he was once again having mental issues and couldn't cope with life.

I remember crying on the plane all the way home, as all I could think about was that he was all alone, with no one to be with him. For me, another terrible guilt trip.

When I was twenty-seven, I traveled to Albuquerque, New Mexico. Returning from dinner to my hotel room, I had this frightening feeling that something terrible had happened.

As I approached the door to my room, I saw a message tucked halfway under the door. It was from Dr. Green, telling me that Father was dying and that I needed to come to Stilwell right away.

I immediately went to the airport and got a ticket to Tulsa, arriving around 9:00 p.m. Unbeknownst to me, a major golf tournament was going on in Tulsa and all the rental cars were leased out.

I broke out crying and begging them to please rent me a car, as my father was dying. A very kind golfer who happened to be there told the people at the desk to lease me his car. I only wish I could have learned his name, but the Lord knows all about his act of kindness.

Shortly after I got onto the highway to drive the ninety miles to Stilwell, fog set in, to the point where I could not see the road unless I felt the tires going off and hitting the gravel on the shoulder. After about a three-hour drive that ordinarily should have taken about an hour and a half, I arrived at the hospital at 3:00 a.m.

I clung to my father and cried and cried, telling him I was there with him and loved him. I'm not sure if he knew, but the doctor assured me that even though he was not conscious, he knew that I was with him.

I stayed next to his bed holding his hand until about ten o'clock the following morning, when Dr. Green insisted that I go to my motel and sleep for a while. He told me that he would call me if anything changed.

About 3:00 p.m., he called to tell me that I should come back, as my father was not doing well. I rushed over to be with him during the last moments of his life.

Daddy died of kidney failure at the young age of sixty-one. Feeling all alone, I called my two aunts and my sister, who informed Mother.

My younger aunt met my sister in Chicago and flew down to Tulsa, where I picked them up and drove back to Stilwell to make the arrangements for burying my father in the family plot.

When I returned to his room in the nursing home, the only thing he had left behind was his Bible on the stand next to his bed and a cigar box filled with his billfold, watch, and comb. I cherished those possessions, even though I didn't have a relationship with the Lord at the time. I think there were two dollars in his billfold.

The pain and loss of my father are beyond my ability to describe, as I loved him so dearly, in spite of the fact that he wasn't there for me most of my life. I know that he loved both my sister and me, but due to his lifelong illnesses he hadn't been able to help or be there for us most of the time.

Family History, Maternal Side

After her brother had died at birth, my mother, an only child, was born into a wealthy family. When only fourteen, her mother ran off with another man.

Growing up, Mother was sent off to summer camps and had her own horse and went to riding school. She spent a lot of her time at resorts and private schools. She graduated from college with a degree in pharmacy.

I never knew much about her childhood, as she refused to talk about it whenever I would bring it up or ask the question. Over the years her bitterness only became worse. I only wish I had known more about her life and family, but that was not to be.

My father and his brother crashed a debutante ball when Father was older, and that is where he met my mother. Tall, dark, and handsome, he swept her off her feet.

The plain truth is that my sister and I were born into a family of bitterness, pain, illness, dysfunction, and constant crisis.

Yes, there were times when you could hear laughter in the house, as we children just naturally gravitated toward the happier moments that could be found in between the cold tension surrounding our mother and father. It was a constant walking on eggshells, hoping that nothing would crack and cause another crisis.

When I was just a small child, my mother's mother came to visit. She immediately took a liking to me, but was very cruel to my older sister, who resembled her with her red hair and fair, freckled complexion.

Grandmother had bought some fingernail polish and proceeded to polish my nails. When my sister ran into the house to Mother and said that Grandma was polishing my nails but wouldn't polish hers, a fight broke out between my mother and grandmother.

They hit each other and struggled for a while, before my mother grabbed my sister and me, and ran out the door toward downtown, where my father was working.

When our parents later came home, they discovered that my grandmother had run off with my mother's fur coat, her jewelry, some other valuables, and my father's picture, of all things.

Later, I was told that a court battle had ensued, and my mother lost all her inheritance from her father. My mother never spoke to her mother again.

When I was in my twenties at a time that I was getting along with my mother, a nursing facility called my mother to tell her that her mother was dying. She hung up on them.

I was flabbergasted to think that she wouldn't even bother to get the name of the place to let my sister or me know about it until later. It broke my heart that she should have harbored such bitterness.

When I asked her which nursing home called, she said that she never asked and didn't want to know. There was nothing that I could do, as Chicago must have a thousand and one nursing facilities.

Honestly, I have never been able to understand all her bitterness. I only wish I had been a Christian back then and could try to see if I could encourage her and lead her to Jesus.

As I grew older and more successful in my careers, I would buy Mother things for her birthday or holidays, only to be told that she didn't like them or wish that I hadn't bought a certain thing, since she wouldn't wear it or use it. Once, on a Mother's Day, I sent her a dozen roses and a card, only to be told that she had thrown them away.

I look back now and realize that my mother actually did many things to help me, which I never appreciated until many years later, when it was too late. I'm sure, just like me, she too wanted to be loved.

When I was twenty-three, I spent more time with her, and although our relationship was one of constant criticism of me on her part, I desperately wanted her approval.

She would brag about me to her friends, but to my face she would only criticize and verbally abuse me. In time, when I underwent therapy, I discovered that it was her way of trying to control me.

Despite her dysfunctional life, Mother was a tireless worker. But she was never given love, nurturing, affirmation, or appreciation for all that she did during her life.

Her willingness to pay for my sister and me to go to private school, buy us clothes, and pay for all our expenses is hard to believe, considering how much abuse she took from my father's side of the family.

Yes, she was bitter, hateful, and angry; but looking back, I now see that she certainly had a right to be in so many instances when she wasn't even a Christian. Most of the abuse came from "Christians."

She hated men, which I can understand, under the circumstances, but if my sister or I went out on a date, she also would call us terrible names concerning our characters.

After my sister or I would break up with boyfriends, she would become friends with them, but during the time we were dating, she both hated them and called us the lowest of names.

When I was sixteen, I went to live with my mother for the summer. She got me a job at a country club. When she got off her job at Abbott Labs, she would work nights with me. Anytime someone would give me a wolf whistle, she would refer to me as "slut," "whore," or other vile names.

We only got along when both of us worked. I spent most of my summer working and at the beach.

My mother was living in a one-bedroom condominium on North Lake Shore Drive in Chicago, which was a rental at the time. One day she called me and told me that they were going to convert the building. You either had to buy your condominium or move out. I purchased the condo for her.

We continued to have many moments of tension, crisis, and criticism, but there were also memorable times when we had some wonderful experiences of sharing, shopping (she was the ultimate shopper), and spending time together.

Then it happened. At the rather young age of 72, my mother was admitted to the hospital with heart disease. I flew to Chicago and rushed over to see her. She was very distraught and agitated. I went to the condo and slept until they called me at 5:00 a.m. to tell me to come over to the hospital, which was right next door, as Mother was dying. Once again, as with Father, I was alone with her when she passed.

One thing my mother would constantly tell me when we had spent time together was, just to mention a few put-downs, "You will be so glad when I am dead" and "Why can't you be a better daughter?"

One time when I flew into Chicago to see her, I took a cab to the condo and rode the elevator up to her apartment. I knocked on the door, and when she opened it; instead of greeting me and giving me a hug, she looked with disdain at me and said, "You didn't wear *that* on the plane, did you?"

The little child in me once again just wanted a hug and positive affirmation from my mom. As usual, it didn't happen.

When she passed, my self- esteem was at an all-time low, with guilt trip after guilt trip, that I wasn't a good daughter to my mother. Tears upon thousands of tears welled up and poured out like rain at her passing.

Many of those tears emerged from unexpressed cries for all the years I wanted to be loved, nurtured, affirmed, hugged, and held in her arms. But it wasn't to be.

Paternal Grandparents

My mother and father had separated when I was four years old. My sister and I were taken from Indiana down to Oklahoma to my father's parents who lived next to an Indian reservation. Grandma was a midwife to the Indians, and Grandpa worked the small farm.

As mentioned earlier, my grandmother was a very strict, legalistic Adventist. I'm sure a lot of her upbringing had much to do with how she viewed the Bible and the Ten Commandments.

Grandma did show us love and would sit with us and read and speak kindly. There were some wonderful, happy memories when my cousins, my sister, and I would play with the dog, pick blackberries, go down the path to get pails of water from the spring, and then return, only to have Grandma check us all over and remove the ticks.

She was an excellent cook and made us very good meals, but each and every plate must be finished before leaving the table.

Grandpa was a very kind and loving person who took time to play with us and sit and hug us as well.

Right before Christmas, approximately six months after my sister and I had moved to Oklahoma, I was sitting in a large metal tub in the kitchen next to the wood stove having my bath, when suddenly the door opened and in walked my father.

I reached out my two little arms yelling "Daddy, Daddy!" He came over, picked me up, dried me off, and dressed me. I was so excited and happy; certain that my daddy was coming to take me home.

Sadly, he went back to Chicago. Once again, he had left my sister and me.

I cried myself to sleep and cannot remember much of anything after that experience down in Oklahoma. I think that was the last time I let my emotions show through tears until I was much older and my father and mother had died. This time marked the beginning of the little child inside of me shutting down all my emotions.

We two sisters returned to the Indiana area and lived in various cities, sometimes with families and sometimes back again with my mom and possibly my father, but I am not sure.

Every time I went to live with another family it resulted in rejection, abandonment, and a certain feeling that I wasn't loved. I acted out my pain in stubbornness, anger, and a determination that no one was ever going to hurt me again. I could take care of myself.

When I was seven and my sister nine, I remember one other time that my father put us on a train in Chicago to send us back down to Stilwell. We had to transfer in Kansas City and then take another train on into Stilwell. How we ever managed it, I don't know. The Lord must have been watching over us, I'm sure.

Once, when Father had brought my sister and me back to live

with them, it felt like a cold had settled into the house. We always had to be so careful what we said or did or Mother would get angry for days on end and never speak, instead displaying this cold, angry, mean demeanor.

You could cut the air with a knife. One time, I remember Father asking me to please go in and kneel down by the bed where Mother was lying, to ask her to forgive us. I never did learn what it was about.

All the while my mother took a tremendous amount of abuse from both of my aunts and my grandmother. You see, my father and his family were "Adventists," and my mother was not!

Sad but true, those three Adventist ladies wrote and said some very abusive, hurtful things to my mother. She was constantly being put down and looked upon as a heathen. It became a constant battle over which of the three would be the most hateful. Tragically, they forgot the love of Jesus in their relationship with my mother. On the other hand, they showed genuine interest for her two young daughters by what they were about to do.

Misadventures in Christian Education

My two Adventist aunts insisted that my sister and I had to go to Adventist schools. Until the last two years before I went to college, I had never gone to any school for more than a year, and sometime only for six months, before ending up in yet another school.

I only went to a public school for one year. That was in the fifth grade. I'm sure that my mother had to work to pay for our Christian education, with help from my two aunts, who did their best to make sure that we had a Christian education.

Around this time, I had shut down most of my emotions. I can honestly say that the only memories of my childhood Adventist education revolve around the stories of Daniel and the lions' den, David and Goliath, and such.

Every time my two aunts would take us to another family willing to room and board in their home while we attended school, they would sit me down on the couch next to them and proceed to explain why my family was such a mess and so dysfunctional.

Little did they realize that my self-worth had become lower and lower. I grew more and more determined not to let anything or anyone hurt me. Inside was a little child whose self-esteem was destroyed, but outside I eventually became a perfectionist, an over-achiever, and a workaholic.

Making friends was never easy or possible for me, as I held everyone at a distance. I was terrified of being abandoned and rejected, and positive that I wasn't loved because no one ever kept me very long.

When it comes to verbal abuse, children can be among the worst tormentors. "Why don't you have a mommy and daddy?" Bullying, constant criticism, and cruel, hurtful taunting were only making my outer shell harder and my attitude more defiant.

On the other hand, my sister was always making friends, and to this day retains a lot of childhood friends. The only friends that I can say I had were the two that I made during my sophomore/junior year.

My aunts taught me to lie at a very young age. "Don't tell your mother you have been with us"; "Don't let anyone know that your father is not well"; and so many others that I eventually reached the point where I became the master of making up stories. "My daddy owns such and such," or "My mother is very wealthy."

I would make up some grandiose things to make it sound like I was somebody important. Dealing with the pain of dysfunction was too much for my young mind to cope with, as opposed to living in a fantasy, pretend world.

I was the child of constant criticism. "You're a bad little girl!" "Why can't you be like your sister?" But all I really wanted was attention and someone to hug me and tell me they loved me. I craved being physically held, something which later led to my life of affairs when I was older.

Of all the families that I lived with, I never remember being nurtured, hugged, or loved. No one affirmed me as a child—just criticism. The more mischief that I got into, the more distant I became as a child.

When I was very little, I lived with a family who owned a home close to a lake. One day their little boy and I were playing near the water with his shovel and pail. He was playing with his truck while I took the pail and filled it with wet sand. He ran over to me and grabbed the pail out of my hands and swung it toward my head, resulting in a gash in my forehead. As with many head wounds, it started to gush blood down onto my face.

He ran home crying, with me close behind. As his mother opened the back door, she looked at me and yelled, "What did you do to my son?" I stood there bleeding profusely, telling her that he had hit me with his pail. Instead of rushing over to comfort or help me, she said that I shouldn't have taken his pail!

Well, she at least took me into the house to clean me up and try to stop the bleeding. I still have the scar to this day.

Later, but still when I was of a young age, I became the victim of lots of different "Me Too" incidents, which I learned to cover up with more lies and buried indifference. More about that later.

When I was in the eighth grade, I went to live with my father's two sisters. My aunts worked as nurses who were "old maids," as they used to call such unmarried women back then.

Many years later, I found out that the younger aunt had been sexually abused by their older brother from her tender age of 8 until she was 11.

When my older aunt went and told their mother what was happening, it was a thing not to be mentioned aloud in the house. Her mother slammed her head against the wall numerous times, slapped her across the head (later causing her to be almost totally deaf in both ears), and commanded her to never say another word to anyone about it.

Since that boy, my father's brother, was the favorite in the family, nothing was done about his behavior, leaving my aunt to suffer the effects of the abuse for many years.

This aunt later turned out to be a brilliant scholar and was a member of the Mensa society. She had a very successful career and was instrumental in setting up the very first computer system to keep track of all medical records back in the fifties.

Unhappily, her childhood abuse and dysfunctional life led to obesity. She became bipolar when she was in her sixties.

While living with my two aunts, I found out something that would later drive me to bury my past along with everything else.

While living with those two aunts during my eighth grade of school, I soon became depressed and obese. They were excellent cooks, but unfortunately, of all the wrong foods. By the time I went off to school, I wore a size 15 dress and weighed 155 pounds.

At the age of 11, I spent the summer being a mother's helper for some wealthy family in the suburbs of Chicago on the North Shore. They had two children, one was two and a half years old, and the other nine months. I would get the children up, bathe, dress, and feed them before cleaning the house spotless. The mother spent all day at the country club, only coming home to check the children in between changing clothes.

That is where I learned that if I were just "perfect" enough, someone would say a kind word or give me a pat on the shoulder.

The parents were amazed at how I could take such good care of their children, clean the house, and work tirelessly—all for the grand sum of eleven dollars a week!

That summer was the only time that I saw my mother's mother. My sister, like me, also worked as a mother's helper, and each of us had a half day off every week on Wednesdays.

We were walking across the street downtown one day, when coming across from the other direction was our grandmother. My sister recognized her, but I didn't have a clue as to who she was.

We approached her, and she invited us into the drugstore on the corner for a soda. I can't remember much of anything other than that she looked old, tired, and stressed. I'm not sure if she ever asked us about our mother. That was the last time that I ever saw my grandmother.

My two aunts decided that my sister and I should go to a school down south that seemed to us like a place a thousand miles away. To me, it was just another way to get rid of us. I hated it from the beginning, and once again had a hard time making friends.

Running late for class one day, I ran down the stairs and twisted my ankle. The sudden pain caused me to involuntarily scream out an unfortunate oath (that verb referring to the mending of socks with holes).

Immediately the dean grabbed me by the cuff of the shoulder and dragged me across the street and up to the principal's office. They both sat there, lecturing me on the evils of cursing and proceeding to make me take a toothbrush and wash my mouth out with soap for the next ten minutes. Sad to say, they never said that Jesus loved me or whether they loved me. Their only concern was my using bad language.

That year I grew four inches taller, lost my baby fat, and had developed into a young woman with endowments that were too much for a little child to bear conveniently and modestly. In fact, I didn't have any clothes that fit and ended up having to borrow clothes from the other girls in the school. My sister went around begging for hand-me-downs, though I was too proud to do that.

Before the year ended, I became a "Me Too" victim by one of the faculty members. I had been learning to play the snare drums, and would go into the music room and beat those drums endlessly, trying to act out my anger and frustration on them.

That summer, my father gave me a snare drum as a gift. It is the only gift that I still have to this day.

At the close of the school year, my sister and I were placed in homes once again to work as mother's helpers. We spent the summer on the beach at Lake Michigan on our days off, the remainder of the time working tirelessly for our respective families.

The next year we were sent to a different school that was closer, but still far from Chicago. That is where I met my two friends who also came from a dysfunctional family. Their father, who was a church elder, would sexually abuse them every Saturday night and throughout the following week.

The three of us were constantly fighting the rules and getting into mischief. It was never anything terrible, in most cases just rebellious.

We had to wear nylons with seams. Instead, we would take an eyebrow pencil and draw a line up the back of our legs, pretending that we were wearing our hose. Most days it worked, but other days, it was back to "free labor."

I spent more time on my knees than any other student. Unfortunately, it wasn't while praying. Instead, it occurred while doing "free labor" as punishment for something that I had said or done wrong.

Back in those days, they used floor polishers called buffers on their waxed floors. On my hands and knees, I had to scrape the wax off the outer edges of the floor with a razor.

Other times, I had to clean and dust all the books in the library. In fact, I was constantly doing "free labor." In contrast, my sister was now a model student and a hall monitor.

I can't remember all the things that I did to bring down the wrath of the dean, but it was always some little thing to upset the apple cart.

Early every day they had morning worship for approximately thirty minutes in the basement of the girls' dorm, while the boys had worship in their own dorm.

When something happened that called for identifying a culprit, they would pass out pieces of paper and tell everyone to write down anything that they personally had done wrong, or had seen someone else do that was wrong.

Many times, the girls would confess something such as, "I took my roommate's socks" or similar types of things.

I hate to say it, but I was determined that there was no way I would ever confess to anything, which had the effect of running the confession sessions into overtime. Eventually, someone would snitch on me about some little thing.

I would be immediately taken to the principal's office, where she would lecture me on the evils of doing whatever thing I did. Once she proceeded to tell me that I was a great leader, but that I led in the wrong direction.

Thinking back about all that "free labor," I never remember them saying anything about the love of Jesus. Their style of discipline seemed an odd way of making disciples, not at all like the patient, redemptive method modeled by Jesus.

Odder still, the faculty never asked me to lead out in reading a Scripture or do anything of a spiritual nature. I was never asked to do anything for the worship services, as only the "good" girls were asked to participate.

I've always felt that if you have dysfunctional, mischievous children, you should put them in charge of something to teach them responsibility. Ask them to be in charge of deciding what the punishment for a child who isn't behaving ought to be. That way, they actually participate in decision making.

For my frequent misdeeds, I was assigned lots of "free labor." How I made it through those misspent school years with good grades is beyond me.

In my junior year, I was presented with a very small portable radio, a gift from my mother. It was about four inches square, small enough to hide in my desk drawer when I wanted to listen to music. I would pin it up behind the drapes while I was out of the room.

But once again, I got caught violating the rules and sent to the principal's office. For this offense, I was going to be suspended for a week. I was taken to the train station and given a ticket to Chicago. Unfortunately, the school officials didn't bother to call my mother, instead calling my Adventist aunts.

The train chanced to stop in a city where I had a casual friend that I had met a long time before. I got off the train and proceeded to spend the night at her place.

My mother just happened to call us that night. That is when it was discovered that I was missing. For some reason, I felt impressed to call my two aunts to let them know I was staying with this friend. In the meantime, they were ready to call the state troopers to see if they could find me.

The next day the school officials informed my aunts and mother that they were going to bring me back to school. I think they were worried about a lawsuit, since I was only fifteen and had been sent home without a chaperone on a train. That would never happen in today's society.

My junior year was the last year that I spent in high school. I went to the University of Illinois the summer afterwards to take some credits in order to get into college.

As expected, my two aunts insisted that I should go to an Adventist college, that was located way down south. I ended up there with a roommate from Japan, whose father was a very wealthy shoe manufacturer. We had nothing in common and seldom saw each other or spoke.

I don't remember anything of that year, other than just studying and going to a concert where the zipper on my dress broke and the entire back of the dress came open! A nice young man was kind enough to cover me up with his coat, while the girls laughed and made fun of me. I wish I could thank him, as he was obviously very well-mannered. I was only seventeen at the time, while everyone else was a year ahead of me.

The next year I went to another Adventist school, where my roommate and I had both come from dysfunctional families. Her uncle was a notorious murderer and her father a pastor.

My very first "love" came into my life that year when I was eighteen and he was twenty-one. He had been in the military for two years. I was a sophomore, and he was a freshman with a delayed start because of his service. Another "Me Too" victim thinking that he loved me. We were engaged, but later that summer he moved to Washington and that was the last I saw of him.

At this juncture, I want to make it very clear that we have some wonderful Christian schools. Just like all churches and schools, there are good and bad people. God is using many wonderful, dedicated teachers and school leaders to bring young people to the Lord. How a child is brought up basically starts with the home. Hopefully, most children are brought up with Godly, dedicated parents who instill in their children the love of Jesus, so that when they go off to school, they will be faithful to the Lord.

Worldly Miseducation
and Its Consequences

When I was nineteen, I moved out to Colorado to be with my aunts. Mother was disappointed, as she had arranged for me to receive a scholarship to college. She had wanted me to go to The University of Michigan, but instead I left and drove out to Colorado, which would be my home from that time onward.

I had worked every year since the age of 11 either as a mother's helper, or eventually, in the country clubs as a waitress. Every holiday, both my sister and I worked. We worked for Thanksgiving, Christmas, New Year's, Easter, and any other holiday.

We never had a holiday at home with families like other folks did. On Christmas, we would work in families' homes serving their Christmas dinners, eating in their kitchens, and cleaning up their dishes.

After I moved out to Colorado to be with my two aunts, they found me a job, once again, as a mother's helper for a very wealthy family. I took care of the children, cleaned the house, and kept everything immaculate.

The family took me with them to Palm Springs, California, for a vacation of a couple weeks. There I met a movie celebrity who asked me out on a date. Little did I know that, once again, it would be a "Me Too" evening. I was nineteen.

That fall, I signed up to attend the University of Denver. My mother agreed to transfer the original scholarship, and I was accepted. But how it must have disappointed her, now alone back in Chicago.

I moved into a dorm with three other girls. I wanted to become a doctor. I thought if I became a doctor, then everybody would think that I was okay.

I started my pre-med courses and soon met a man who was much older, and who wanted me to move to an apartment as opposed to living in the dorm. Impetuously, I moved out and became involved in what I will call an "affair." My life had by now taken on an entirely different tone, as I had no desire to have anything to do with "religion."

Now I discovered the world of money, power, success, and living for the pleasures of self. Throughout my careers I lived off the adrenalin of success.

All my life, I had looked at myself as ugly, bad, and never going to be good enough. When men became attracted to me, my immaturity, along with my low self-esteem, constantly denied that I might be okay or maybe even pretty. Ironically, until I was old, I honestly never considered that I was pretty.

My grades started to slip. I was called into the dean's office, where he told me that I had rated in the top ten on scholastic scores, but I was not applying myself to my studies. I promised to study more.

Shortly thereafter, I moved into another apartment complex, where I met the next man in my life, who turned out to be one year younger than I.

Mark was a brilliant law student who lived across from me in the next apartment building. We had met at the pool. While he was a junior in school, I was a senior, despite my average grades.

He was studying to be a lawyer. His family owned or leased from the government forty square miles of land in what is known as the Middle Park alpine region of Colorado. They were Hereford cattle ranchers. We became engaged that spring, and were planning a fall wedding.

We had spent a tremendous amount of time skiing in Vail during our winter quarter, as Mark was an excellent skier. He had grown up with Buddy Werner, an Olympic ski racer who tragically died in an avalanche in the Swiss Alps. He and Buddy had been good friends, skiing together while growing up. Eventually, I became a very good skier as well.

Unfortunately, Mark was a beer drinker and a smoker. He could easily put away a six-pack of beer and smoked about a pack and a half a day.

Approximately two years earlier, his sister had been killed in a car accident. His mother was an alcoholic, telling him when his sister had died that she wished he had been the one.

Mark was an avid reader and a brilliant young man; however, he also had low self-esteem. His parents owned the only bank in Kremmling, about 100 miles west of Denver, and deposited $5,000 into his checking account every month.

But Mark would be overdrawn many months, as he was always

"buying" for his friends in trying to act the big shot. As you might imagine, he had a lot of friends in college who loved to go drinking with him!

That summer I got a job in the hotel industry, and Mark and I took up housekeeping together. His folks were all excited about the fall wedding, and were planning on renting the main hotel in Steamboat Springs for the weekend. It was going to be a three-day party with all expenses paid for the wedding, including the guests' accommodations, food, and beverages.

I started my job at the Hilton Hotel as a secretary to the director of food and beverage, but it was only out of desperation that they hired me at all.

The catering manager had had an affair with his secretary, resulting in a pregnancy. He was fired along with the secretary; and the director of food and beverage also quit at the same time.

The new director of food and beverage had just been hired himself, so when I applied, he asked me if I had any experience in food and beverage. I told him that I had taken "Foods and Nutrition" when I was in college, so he hired me. I *honestly* don't recall now that I had taken any such course.

I typed about thirty words a minute, with as many mistakes. He later decided to put me into the sales department, as I had demonstrated a great gift of gab.

We all got along great, and I fell in love with the hotel business. I would work twelve or fourteen hours a day, and loved every aspect of booking the catering functions for the conventions, and scheduling help for the banquets and the seven restaurants.

I did all the forecasting and became very successful in coming up with marketing themes for the convention banquets. I received many letters from corporations thanking me for the outstanding banquets and parties that they held during their conventions.

As all this was going on, Mark and I found less and less time together. I told him that we should wait until he graduated from law school before we got married, which made his parents very upset; but Mark said that he would wait until after he graduated.

Mark and I broke up for the last time shortly after his graduation. He graduated top of his class and set a precedent at the very first case he ever tried. He was the president of the Colorado Bar Association. We remained friends, but he died an alcoholic with multiple sclerosis.

My boss at the hotel was offered a job in San Francisco with the Marriott Corporation. I would outlast five food and beverage directors afterwards. By the time the last one came on board, they asked me to train him. I was doing all the work. He would come in around 11:00 a.m., go to lunch in one of the restaurants, and then leave around four or five.

Most of the banquets were in the evenings, leaving me to stay on to make sure everything was okay. When they fired this last food and beverage director, I went to the general manager of the hotel and told him that I wanted to apply for the job, as I was doing all the work anyway, including the training of new people.

He openly stated, "We don't hire women for management positions." Back in those days, hotels would hire women as desk clerks, maids, waitresses, and housekeepers, but never in a management position. Without thinking, I said, "I quit," and that was it. I picked up my things and left.

Two days later, the director of sales and marketing called me from the hotel, stating that he had a friend who was opening another major hotel two blocks down from the Hilton and that he would try to help me get the job as director of sales and marketing.

I had never been involved in the sales and marketing of conventions before, but I applied for the job and was hired. Because I was the first female director of sales and marketing for a major hotel in Denver, they did an article in the newspaper, and thus began my positions as the first female in many careers down through the years. Our hotel started out with 100% occupancy for many months, along with boasting the hottest nightclub in the city.

I was constantly getting awards for sales and marketing, and became involved in the hotel sales and marketing organization. I was the first female president of the organization and was awarded a citation from the mayor of Denver for outstanding sales and marketing, amounting to over two million dollars worth of sales in a year. That was a lot of money back in those days.

Once again, I met a man who was to be a large influence in my life over the next fifty-two years. He came into the hotel and asked to see a sample room. I thought he had meant a sample *of* a room.

We started at the top of the hotel and worked our way downward as I showed him all the various types of rooms, from suites to king size to two queens, until we finally got down to the second floor, where we had breakout rooms.

He said, "This is what I need. I'm in the men's sportswear business, and I need a room to show my lines." We laughed, as I asked him why he kept letting me show him all the other types of rooms. He said he just liked to watch me walk down the halls! We would remain the best of friends until his death in 2020.

Shortly after the room demonstration episode, I was asked to teach a course at the University of Colorado in "Professional Women in Sales and Marketing." It was an evening class, so it didn't take away from my other job. Once again, I was written up in the newspaper with a headline story: "Barbara Taylor is motivated to succeed."

Now I was asked to become the director of sales and marketing at the Radisson Hotel. We had a tremendous number of entertainers and celebrities staying there when they were filming movies or having concerts. My life would now be filled with parties and a totally wrong lifestyle type.

After eight years in the hotel business, my life was about ready to take a big turn.

The *True* Cost of Fame and Fortune

My boss at the hotel had jokingly told two executives that it was a good thing they weren't looking for a woman to be their first director of club relations for Playboy International. This set a course whereby I was called and asked to come to Chicago to be interviewed for that very job.

After three days of interviews and testing, I was offered the job of being the first female director of club relations for Playboy International. I would later become the first general manager for Playboy International.

As the first female GM, I was interviewed by all the major television and radio stations, newspapers, and magazines, and was even mentioned by Johnny Carson and Buddy Hackett on *The Tonight Show*. *Time* magazine ran an article, and I was in 841 newspapers around the world.

Tragically, and not too surprisingly, I became involved in the lifestyle of the rich and famous, excusing everything I did by convincing myself that I was up there with the "in-crowd."

Going to all the "in" parties with celebrities thrust me into the environment of drugs and drinking. I met a very wealthy man who showered me with gifts, jewelry, fur coats, and trips around the world. Everything was first-class from Las Vegas to Beverly Hills to Aspen, and wherever there was a party or gathering.

With my marketing background, I was able to turn the sagging profits of the Playboy clubs into a net profit.

If you are familiar with many radio and television sports talk shows today, they are a direct result that a friend and I devised. He came to me one day and asked if we could host a Denver Bronco player and a sportswriter over lunchtime once a week to talk sports and answer questions.

Thus began the Playboy Sports Backtalk series. On Monday we would have the Colorado University Football Club luncheon with the head coach, Tuesday was Colorado State University, Wednesday was the Bronco luncheon with a top player and sportswriter, Thursday was the Falcon Quarterback Club with their head coach from the Air Force Academy, and Friday was a lunch with Football Funnies or some highlight film.

The first week we had just a few people attend, but soon after it was always a packed house. Later, when I left Playboy, two sports celebrities asked me what I thought about having a radio program where they would just talk sports for an hour and take questions from the listeners. I thought it was a great idea. Thus began the era of sport talk radio and TV shows across the country.

Behind the lifestyle of many celebrities was a tremendous emptiness that they tried to fill with drugs, parties, and overachievement—all to make sure that they stayed up there with the in-crowd.

Their greatest fear was that they would slip into oblivion in the ratings. Many became addicted to their drugs, alcohol, and narcotics, which too often ended in death.

Very few of the celebrities ever really had close friends or relationships, but instead surrounded themselves with groupies who would be at their beck and call.

I won't describe the lifestyle of many of them, as it is so very deplorable and difficult to imagine how low mankind can stoop right down into Satan's pit.

After three and a half years, I was totally burned out. My dear friend Ed came into the club one night and asked me if I would consider coming to work for a men's sportswear company that was owned by General Mills. The latter owned five apparel and jewelry companies, including Izod, FootJoy, Monet, Lord Jeff of Amherst, and one other company that I no longer recall.

Lord Jeff was a men's sportswear company that sold men's sweaters. Because they were going to add slacks to the line, my friend had to give up that line to prevent a conflict with his Sansabelt slack line.

Lord Jeff employed 27 salesmen. I was their first female sales rep. Within three years, I became the number one sales rep. The fourth year four other gentlemen and I bought the company from General Mills and took it from a nine-million-dollar company to a 48-million-dollar company. We were the largest domestic sweater company in the United States.

We did private labeling for all the major stores and catalogs, as well as our own label. Regrettably, the man who owned 51% of the company and I began an affair. As soon as he found out about my celebrity friends, he wanted to meet them. Instead of getting out of the lifestyle, I was right back into it. We were both workaholics, laboring through fourteen- to sixteen-hour days and partying all weekend.

I commuted every other week from Denver to Manhattan, had a limo pick me up and take me to the showroom at 5 East 51st Ave., right across from St. Patrick's Cathedral, or take me to the plant in Norwood, New Jersey.

Bob was an outstanding salesman, but unfortunately not a good businessman. His life see-sawed between fantasy and crisis. Whenever he had a crisis, he would find someone to blame instead of taking personal responsibility. He would call me immediately and tell me that I had to help him with the crisis. I loved responsibility and taking care of things, so that fit me to a tee. However, as soon as the crisis was over, he would flip back into fantasy and never deal with reality.

If a buyer came in and mentioned liking a certain sweater, Bob would immediately tell production to put in lots of dozens of that exact style. He didn't wait to receive a purchase order, which many times never came.

Instead of waiting to get feedback from the salesmen as to what was selling and to gauge production accordingly, he would overproduce everything, which caused us to experience a crisis at the end of each season.

After eight and a half years of constant traveling, exhausting work, and partying, I was burned out, unhappy, and looking for answers in all the wrong places.

Near the end of our business relationship, we had three cottage industries overseas in Ireland, England, and Scotland, which made hand-knit sweaters for us. We would go over to the UK and put certain patterns into our sample line and later return there to finalize which ones would go into the line.

In the meantime, we were becoming more and more involved again in all the wrong lifestyles.

Toward the end of the eight and a half years, we hired a 29-year-old girl to work with us in merchandizing. She was married to a young man working on his master's degree, and they were just starting out their lives together.

One day when I was in the plant and waiting for a limo to pick me up and take me to the airport, she asked if she could get a ride to the Brooklyn Bridge, as she had no car and always had to take the subway home.

When she got into the car, she started telling me that she loved my fur coats, jewelry, Gucci purses, and all my designer clothes. She said, "I am going to find me a 'sugar daddy' to buy me nice things." I was shocked, told her that Chuck was such a nice young man, and asked why she would do something like that.

We were scheduled to go over to England, Ireland, and Scotland in October to set the patterns for the following season. I told Bob that I was exhausted and that he should go over with the other people in merchandizing to set the patterns—a group that included this girl—and that we would go over in January to finalize the styles.

To make a long story short, Bob and the girl had an affair while they were in Scotland. When he called me and sounded different, I knew instantly. It almost sounded like a little child who had gotten caught with his hand in the cookie jar. This dismal episode was the beginning of a downward spiral in my life, his life, and the company's life.

I'm sure that the girl thought she had found her sugar daddy and that life was going to be filled with lots of gifts. What she didn't realize was that Bob was a narcissist who spent money only on his own pleasures. If it involved something that brought him pleasure, money was not an object; but when it came to lavishing gifts, that was another story.

Because Bob owned 51% of the company and I only owned 12½ %, he shut me out of the business. We were privately owned, so I had no recourse, nor could I force him to buy me out.

I still had to go into the office and work, as I had no other means of income. It was like having a man's mistress come and live with you in your own home.

My mother died the summer before this all happened. As I mentioned earlier, I was alone with her when she passed. I can't explain the guilt trip that I felt while actually believing all the verbal abuse that she cast at me over the years. I blamed myself constantly for not being a "good enough" daughter.

Back at the plant, everyone knew what had happened. For me personally, it produced the constant nightmare of living in denial. This certainly couldn't be happening to me. I had always been determined that no one was going to hurt me.

I had always been a self-confident woman inside my business world persona, but when this happened, the little child in me that had been terrified of being abandoned, rejected, and unloved went into a deep depression marked by a total lack of self-esteem. I had just gone from being a multimillionaire to near bankruptcy. Every day I would drive over to my office in Denver and cry and cry.

One day as I was crying and driving to my office, I remembered a song from my childhood—"Jesus Loves Me." I couldn't remember the rest of the song, but would hold onto the steering wheel and cry and cry, saying over and over, "Jesus loves me, this I know. Jesus loves me, this I know."

Some Christian Witnesses!

One Sabbath I decided to go to church. I had been crying all night and had swollen, red eyes and a puffy nose from blowing it. I got up, dressed, and tried to cover up my face with makeup so that it wasn't so noticeable.

I went into a large church with about eight hundred and fifty members at the time. The lady at the door looked right at me and said, "Good morning," handed me a church bulletin, and never said another word.

As I walked in and sat down, no one ever greeted or welcomed me, but sat stone silent right next to me. After the church service was over, they all greeted and talked to one another, but no one spoke to me.

I stormed out of the church telling myself that I was never coming back, as they were nothing but a bunch of hypocrites. As I later discovered, that's what we are, that's why we are in church.

About three weeks went by, and I was becoming totally suicidal. One of my celebrity friends had me talk to his psychiatrist, who lived in Aspen but had another office in Manhattan.

I had been crying all night once again, and when I got up, I called him and told him to put me in the hospital because I was going to kill myself. We talked for about an hour, as I cried and cried. He said that I should call him on Monday, and we would talk some more in his Manhattan office, as I happened to be scheduled to fly into New York.

When I was with Playboy, my two aunts had come to visit me and asked me to go to church with them. I reluctantly agreed. We went to a church that was further away toward the west of the city.

Can you imagine what I must have looked like that Sabbath? I was a size 8 and had tight, short dresses, spiked high heels, about $75,000 worth of jewelry, and enough makeup that if you hit the back of my head, my face would have fallen off!

Looking back, I would love to have had a video of what the church members must have said, or how they looked at me when I came in that day. When it came to jewelry, I was the Mr. T back then. I didn't and still don't remember much of what the pastor said.

After talking with the doctor that morning, I decided that I would get up, wash my face in cold water, and try to go to that church.

Once again, as I passed through the door, there was a lady who looked directly at my face, handed me a church bulletin, said, "Good morning," and never said another word.

I walked into the church, which was an octagonal building with four sections of pews, and sat in the corner seat at the end of one of the long pews.

A tiny little lady sitting at the opposite end of the pew looked over at me and noticed that I had been crying. She didn't really have a reason to get up, but thank the Lord, she did. She came over to where I was sitting and put her hand on mine and asked me if I was okay. I began to cry again.

At that point in my life, I so desperately needed the kindness in a human touch. She was so kind and stayed with me throughout the entire service.

On the back of the pew was a tithe envelope and a form on which you could write your name and phone number if you wanted someone to call or contact you. I wrote down my name and number and put it into the tithe envelope when they took up the offering. But no one called!

Once again, I was positive that I would never go back to those churches, as no one seemed to care. But God sees the "big picture"; we just see the little picture. He must have known that I wasn't ready yet.

One thing that I did learn from the psychiatrist involved the idea of intimate love. He had written a book on "Zones," explaining that there are four zones: Business, Social, Personal, and Intimate.

"You have your business zone, where you go to work, do a great job, and then leave for the cocktail party, which is your social zone. You visit, socialize, and say all the right things. You meet a man who invites you to dinner. You have dinner together, which is your personal zone. After dinner he invites you up to his hotel room where you make love. What zone are *you* in?"

Of course, I said, "Intimate." He explained that even animals have sex. But the intimate zone is when two people have a relationship that is honest, mutually trusting one another to be able to confide in each other without it going any further. They support and give positive affirmations to one another. They never put one another down in front of others. You can count on them to be there for you no matter what the circumstances. They are honest and open about their love for you each and every day. There were about ten different things that he listed, but these are just a few.

You see, as a child, I had never been shown or taught about healthy love. When you come from a dysfunctional lifestyle, you automatically drift toward others who are dysfunctional. You think that what you experience is normal, even though it is not.

Growing up, I always ended up with dysfunctional men who were full of empty holes, just as I was. Thinking that we were going to fill each other's empty holes only resulted in more messed-up relationships. Kind of like the Swiss -cheese effect. Except when you put the two slices together, they don't fit into a whole piece of solid cheese.

Things were getting progressively worse in my life. Bob was cold and indifferent. As much as he once loved me, he now was just the opposite.

Sad to report, after he shut me out of the business, he and the young lady designed a line of short sleeve woven shirts, available in over fifty-two patterns, with four to six colors per style. The result was the beginning of the eventual bankruptcy of what was once a great company.

No matter what I said, he would get very angry and say that I didn't know what I was talking about. Within two years the company went from a $48 million business to a $27 million business with a $6 million loss.

I was trying to hold on for dear life to all my real estate and my income, but if things didn't turn around soon, I was looking at bankruptcy myself.

Once again, I was crying all night and wanted to just end it all. I remembered the kind little church lady and thought, *Maybe I will just try to go to that church one more time.*

The very same scenario occurred when I walked in, with another little lady saying, "Good morning," looking me straight in the face, and never saying another word.

I walked into the sanctuary with my head down, and just as I turned into the pew, who do you think was sitting at the opposite end? You guessed it.

Once again, she had no particular reason to get up, but she did anyway. When she came over and touched my hand, I immediately began to cry and told her that no one had contacted me the previous time.

She felt very bad and said that she would take me to the pastor after church and introduce me to him. It turned out to be the associate pastor.

Thus began my journey in becoming a Seventh-day Adventist Christian. You might be asking yourself, *Wasn't Barbara Taylor a Seventh-day Adventist when she lived with those families or went to the schools?* You need to realize that I was a bitter little child who wasn't about to let anything or anyone get too close to me. I looked at God as a critical parent I could never please, so why even try?

I can honestly say that I was so bitter and angry with God that I don't remember much of anything religiously. I shut my mind against all religious thoughts and was determined that I could take care of myself. If only I had realized the truth early in my life, what a difference it would have made!

After the kind lady introduced me to the associate pastor, I went home that day still not totally convinced that that is what I really needed in my life if things were going to turn around.

One Friday night I was sitting on my back deck, which overlooked the lake where I lived, when I heard someone call out my name. It was the associate pastor. He had rung the doorbell, but since I was outside on the deck, I didn't hear it. Seeing me sitting outside, he had climbed up onto the large rocks next to the deck and called out my name.

After I let him inside, we went back outside on the deck, where I poured out my heart to him about what I had been through. Tears, tears, and more tears. He was very kind and just let me talk for about an hour.

I began Bible studies with him over the next few weeks, and I slowly began to realize the peace and assurance that only Christ could bring into my life.

At the same time, a friend of mine came into my office one day and mentioned that her husband, who was in the import/export business, was overwhelmed with the sudden great demand for latex gloves. This was at the time when the first outbreak of AIDS had begun. She asked me if I would consider starting such a business with them.

When I had taught the "Professional Women in Sales and Marketing" course at the University of Colorado, I told the students that you needed to have four "N's" to succeed in business. First you had to have a Need, next you had to have a Niche, then a Net profit. The fourth N was knowledge (where phonics trumps spelling!).

After doing a lot of research, I discovered that 52% of all women purchase condoms. When they go into a store's feminine hygiene section, they may pick up both their feminine products and a package of condoms. Most of the products had very masculine names like Trojan, Ramses, and Sheik.

My girlfriend and I started the latex company and spent six months researching everything from the products side, as well as the marketing side. We named our company "BARLO" (BA for Barbara, R for Robin, and LO for Lonnie, Robin's husband).

Our design depicted a rainbow type of spectrum on a white background. We named the product "FOR-US" adding "With your protection in mind" as a subtitle.

Within six months, our test market in drugstores and grocery stores was outselling the major brands in some areas. The buyer for a major drugstore chain told us that in all 27 years as a buyer, Carter-Wallace (Trojan's manufacturer) had never requested a brochure from a competitive brand until our product came out.

We were in the process of raising the necessary funds to launch the product nationwide in January, and things looked like we were on the road to success in a multimillion-dollar industry.

In the meantime, I met with the pastor and mentioned that I was starting a new business. When he asked me about the business and I told him latex gloves and condoms, he simply said, "Why don't you just pray about it?" He never criticized me or acted shocked.

If more of our church members would say similar things when someone does or says something that might seem to go against the grain, we would have a lot more members in our pews today.

About this time, my partners announced that they were going to have a baby. They had tried for three years without success and were very excited to be able to have a child.

Robin was the detail person, I was the sales and marketing person, and Lonnie took care of production. I wasn't opposed to this arrangement, as I loved traveling and selling products.

About a week or two before Thanksgiving, one of my celebrity friends called me and invited me to come up to Aspen over Thanksgiving weekend, as all the celebrities would be in town for the big parties.

When I went to study the Bible with the pastor, I once again mentioned that I might be going up to Aspen to spend the weekend with my friends. I hadn't told my celebrity friends that I was studying the Bible, let alone the Sabbath. Once again, he simply said, "Why don't you pray about it?"

Dive Loop on Life's Roller Coaster

Obviously, I didn't pray hard enough. The Holy Spirit was trying to tell me that I shouldn't go near that lifestyle again, then Satan would tell me that it would be just fine.

At that time of year, the sun goes down early. Satan said that I could safely go up to see my friends, and the parties would not start until after sundown Saturday night. I could just relax and not say anything about the Sabbath, and then after sundown, I could go see all my friends at the parties.

I spent Wednesday and Thursday skiing and having Thanksgiving dinner with my friends up at Copper Mountain. I woke up Friday morning, looked out the window at the sun shining, snow on the ground, and thinking maybe I would go over "just this once."

I called my celebrity friend, telling her that I would be leaving and coming over for the weekend. It was 10:00 a.m., and that was the last thing that I remember.

I had a car from General Motors when I appeared in a full-page ad for Tilt-Wheel Steering, which ran in 19 national magazines such as *People*, *Newsweek*, *Time*, *Reader's Digest*, *Sports Illustrated*, and all the other top magazines in the country. The ad with my handwritten testimonial under a photo of me behind the wheel ran twice throughout the year.

My Pontiac Grand Prix boasted a sporty low front end, sunroof, velour seats, and all the bells and whistles. I was ten miles outside of Aspen at 1:50 p.m., when I was hit head on by a

Chevrolet Suburban. My car flipped over two and a half times, the engine was pushed up into where the front seat had been, and, still locked in my seat belt, I was near where the back seat was located.

The good news is that I don't remember a thing about the accident. I didn't have to worry how I was going to spend the Sabbath *that* weekend, as I didn't regain consciousness until Sunday.

It took two and a half hours to cut me out of the car. I had a concussion, shattered metal and glass imbedded in my skull, a broken nose, a severed lip that was dangling by a piece of tissue, and all my teeth had been pushed up into my gums. Eventually, I lost the two front teeth.

In addition, my sternum was crushed and there were contusions in my heart and lungs. I also suffered kidney damage, broken bones in my hand, and both knees were the size of basketballs.

The worst fracture was to my right foot. It was so badly damaged that they couldn't get a bone definition. They said it was like a baked potato that had been squished.

One of the men who owned the top restaurant in Aspen served on the volunteer fire department. We had partied together the previous year at the Super Bowl game. He helped cut me out of the car, somehow recognizing me in the process.

After he helped cut me out of the car, he called my celebrity friend and told her that he didn't think I would survive. She immediately went to the hospital. When she saw the gurney covered in blood, she called another celebrity friend, who flew in thinking that I was going to die.

God had other plans for me.

Answered Prayers
and Miracles

Five orthopedic doctors in Aspen insisted that they had to amputate my foot. It was so badly crushed that they said I could easily have a blood clot and die.

Requiring 53 stitches, one of the plastic surgeons stitched my bottom lip back on, and helped reset my nose until I could undergo surgery to rebuild it.

When they insisted on amputating my foot, all I can remember saying to the doctors through my swollen lip was "No! No! NO!"

They put a morphine pump in my chest and kept me heavily sedated. Every other day they would wheel me into surgery to remove more imbedded metal and glass from my skull. Every day they insisted on having to amputate my foot, and every day I kept insisting "No! No! NO!"

After 26 days in the hospital, I was transferred to Swedish Hospital, where the doctor who was head of orthopedic surgery at CU Medical Center, said that he did not think anything could be done for my foot. But if it were his foot, he admitted, he would go see Dr. Roger Mann in San Leandro, California, who was the leading foot orthopedic surgeon in the world.

The CU orthopedic surgeon added that it would probably take up to six months to get in to see Dr. Mann, as he was in such high demand. I called the pastor and asked him to pray for me and to anoint my foot, which was done.

I then phoned Dr. Mann's office and was put on hold. When the nurse came back on the line, I explained my situation. She said that the lady who was at that moment on the other line while I was on hold had just canceled her appointment and that I could come in at the end of the month. A clear answer to prayer!

With all my casts and crutches, they put me on a plane to California. Dr. Mann was very nice, and after about two and a half hours of tests and questions, he came back into my room and told me that he had good news and bad news.

The good news was that he was going to rebuild my foot. The bad news was that I would have to wait from nine months to a year to allow all the nerve and tissue damage to quiet down inside, before they could perform the first of five surgeries.

Exactly one year after my first appointment, I flew out to San Leandro for what was to be the first of five surgeries, beginning at the base of my heel and proceeding down through my foot and into my toes.

Five years later I had a foot that I could walk on, but I was unable to move it up and down, wiggle my toes, or rotate my ankle. Dr. Mann said that rebuilding my foot was one of the most difficult surgeries he had ever performed. Surely, God had been with him, guiding him throughout.

Eventually, another doctor rebuilt my nose with nine bone grafts from a cadaver. An oral surgeon took cartilage out of the roof of my mouth, rebuilt my gum line, and inserted a bridge.

Some wonderful news was that after my first foot surgery and six months of healing, I was carried into the baptismal pool at church and finally baptized.

My two aunts, who would always tell me that they loved me and were praying for me, were able to witness my baptism before they died, for which I thank the Lord every day.

Yes, like me, my aunts were dysfunctional from childhood. I just pray that they were able to submit to the Lord and repent of all their sins before falling asleep in death. They died six hours apart from each other. Once again, I was alone with them at the time.

My motto used to be, as Lee Iacocca would say: "Either Lead, Follow, or Get Out of the Way!" Now my motto is: "Jesus Leads, I Follow, and Let Me Love and Help Others Along the Way!"

I wish it were easy to bring my story to a close on a good note right here. But there is more to tell.

Ups and Downs,
Twists and Turns

Once I was baptized, I was on fire to share the Gospel with others for the Lord, beginner's mistakes and all.

For those reading this, remember one thing: Satan doesn't pay much attention to those who are lost. He puts all his efforts and evil angels to work on those who have accepted Jesus into their lives.

Growing up as a street kid with street smarts, but not a whole lot of common sense, I wanted to be in control and take charge instead of letting God and His Holy Spirit lead me and point me in the right direction. To this day, it remains one of my greatest challenges.

Due to my five years of surgeries and no one to do the fundraising or marketing, once again, another friend approached me with a project after we had lost the condom company.

I later found out that Carter-Wallace, the largest condom company that had requested our brochure from one of the largest drugstore buyers, had gotten their board together and decided to put out a product to counter ours.

They spent half a million dollars on a package that, as I recall, depicted the silhouette profile of a lady sitting in a cane back armchair with head downcast and eyes closed. They named this product "Trojan–For Her." That is like absurdly implying "Tampax–For Him"! Needless to say, it didn't go anywhere. Had I known, I would have been happy to sell our name and packaging to them for the half million dollars.

Shortly after my last surgery, my friend showed me a product called a "Cordminder" which had been invented by an elderly gentleman who was a brilliant inventor but horrible businessman. (We will call him Tim.)

He was the gentleman who had invented the original backup alarm that you see (and hear!) in all equipment to alert others that the apparatus is backing up. Disgustingly, his son stole the patent and wanted nothing to do with his father afterwards. It's too long a story to tell here. This incident was simply dreadful, needless to say.

The Cordminder company was struggling, as Tim simply could not understand mass production. He had been taking the money and building one Cordminder, selling it, then building another one, all by hand.

He had the ability to manufacture approximately a thousand a week, but certainly not enough ability to go nationwide without automation.

Well, Tim asked me to fly over to Boise to talk with him about running the company. I agreed to become the president and to commute from Denver to Boise every week.

The Cordminder was a little bigger than a quarter around and an inch thick over its eight-foot length, or about the size of a silver dollar for the 16-foot length model.

The cord was flat and would rewind into the holder, doing away with all the unsightly, twisted, dirty telephone cords attached from the phone handle to the phone base, such as you might find in a regular cord.

Had everything gone as planned, we would have enjoyed a good five-year run. (Nowadays, most phones are wireless, but that was certainly not the case back then.)

We began selling Cordminders in warehouses, hardware stores, and many other places with great success, but very little profit, as Tim's people had made a bad agreement with two men prior to my becoming the president. I decided to put together a marketing plan for the sales force to receive a 10% commission, which would help to reduce the costs.

One of Tim's "pals," a so-called engineer, had convinced him to let his son take $100,000 worth of the product at no cost. He told Tim that his son would pay him back once he sold the product. He was selling them for $8.95 and $10.95, and never paid back a penny. This foolish arrangement would eventually prove to be fatal.

After a few months at the plant, I decided to fly into New Jersey, where AT&T was headquartered. I aimed to see if they might consider taking on the product as one of their brands.

I flew into New York, going out to New Jersey to meet with John, the VP of marketing and sales. I showed him the product and demonstrated how it could eliminate the unsightly, unsanitary cords on any regular phone.

He took a look at it and then handed it back to me. He said that he didn't think they would be interested, as it didn't meet the standards of an AT&T product. I was devastated.

I offhandedly asked him to just give me another minute. He smiled, took in a deep breath, and said, "Okay." I then asked him if he would be willing to tell me what needed to be done to possibly bring it up to an AT&T standard.

Once again, he took in a deep breath and said, "Okay." He listed things that we would need to do, and said that if we could accomplish those things, he would send it over to their laboratory and let me know if it was approved.

I couldn't wait to get back to Boise to tell them that we might have a chance to get the product approved, based on the items that needed to be done. Tim and the factory staff went to work right away on each listed item.

Just as I came in one morning, Tim asked me to come into his office. He said that he didn't want to continue with the company. He asked me if I would take over the company, which I agreed to do on the basis that I would give him $5 million for the company (which is what he had already invested), as well as have him stay on as a consultant with a 10% commission on anything new that we might develop.

The actual wire that was developed was worth a lot more than the entire Cordminder business. It would take too long here to go into all the details, but soon afterward his attorney and my attorneys drew up the agreement to purchase the patents and the business.

I began what is known as "dialing for dollars" by putting out feelers for anyone who might be interested in investing in the company to get it automated for manufacturing our product.

Happily, I soon received a call from John at AT&T, who informed me that they had approved the product to take it nationwide. He assured me that we wouldn't need a sales force, as they owned all the key retail spaces in all the stores across North America.

I went across the street to the factory and announced the good news, plus the fact that I would be purchasing the company. I then explained that I was an Adventist and that we would be going to a four-day workweek, Monday through Thursday.

In the meantime, I put into the agreement that at the closing the son of the engineer would have to pay the $100,000 that he owed Tim.

After many calls and meetings, I found an investor who was willing to put up the five million for 35% of the business.

Just before the date of the closing, I went to Denver to meet with the investor. Due to a fog that had settled over Boise, I was unable to return for two days.

Tim started calling me and asking why he didn't show a large amount of money in his checking account. I tried to explain that his accountant had written checks that exceeded the amount he had in his account.

He still could not understand. I tried to simplify it by telling him that if he had a dollar in his hand and an invoice for one dollar that he would have to give over the dollar. He still insisted that he should see the money in his checking account. That comment sent up a red flag.

When I finally returned to Boise, Tim was not in the office. I met with some vendors, and shortly after they left, the engineer walked in and told me that Tim had backed out of the sale. He abruptly told me to collect my things and leave without any further discussion.

To say the very least, I was shocked. But instead of calling my attorney, I went to the apartment I had been renting and spent the weekend thinking that Tim would call anytime and say that this was all just a mistake.

Meanwhile, unbeknownst to me, the engineer had convinced Tim that since AT&T was going to take and run with the Cordminder, they didn't need to sell the company after all. He had no clue that the product would have to be automated to accomplish this.

I called to talk with John at AT&T, explaining what had happened. His secretary answered the phone to tell me that John had had a massive heart attack and wouldn't be coming back to the company.

Looking back on everything, I realized that had everything gone as planned, I probably would have backslidden into being a workaholic, overachiever, and perfectionist, leaving no time for the Lord.

Success was the adrenaline in my life. You see, every week I would fly into Boise, work endless hours, and leave on Friday afternoon to arrive in Denver around shortly before sundown.

My nephew and his wife, who were not Adventists, would pick me up. I would take them to dinner before going home to unpack. Many times, the sun had already gone down.

But the business of the past week was still running through my mind. The Lord knew that I would be going down a wrong path toward destruction.

The Cordminder business went bankrupt shortly afterward, and Tim passed away a couple of years later. The entire business venture had failed.

Planting a Church

After what happened in Boise, I went through a time of depression and discouragement. I realized that I had not been faithful to the Lord.

For those of you who might be workaholics, you are burying yourself in your work in most cases, so as not to deal with issues in your life. It might be your personal life, your family life, or some other issue that you want to bury or deny.

Without a good balance between your devotional life with the Lord and quality time with your family, in trying to deal with emotional issues that you may have buried since childhood, you can never find complete hope, certainty, or assurance for the future without God's leading.

The hardest thing for me to deal with was realizing that I could only make myself whole by submitting my life completely to the Lord. I was just one of those self-dependent individuals. As I went through intensive soul-searching and praying to the Lord on my knees one night, I pleaded with Him to use me as He willed, asking Him, "What would You have me to do"?

Back came the answer in a voice as clear as I'm sharing this with you, saying: "Plant a church at Copper Mountain."

For years I had owned my ski condo at Copper Mountain and would go up to ski and party all weekend. At the time I was living in a 3,300 square-foot home in Centennial, a suburb of Denver.

I drove up to Copper Mountain one week and spoke with the then-president of the Copper Mountain Chapel Foundation, asked her if I could rent the chapel for our church service. She said that they already had the Copper Mountain Community Church, and the Christian Science, Unitarian, and Catholic churches that all met for an hour each on Sundays, so she didn't know if there would be another hour available for us to meet.

I was glad to explain that our congregation met on Saturdays! She told me that they had weddings on Saturdays, but would ask the board if we could meet. I explained that we would need the chapel from 9:00 a.m. until 2:00 p.m., as we would be having Sabbath School, church, and fellowship lunch activities each week.

Praise the Lord, after sharing my "abbreviated" testimony with the then-Community Church pastor, he convinced the board that we should be able to meet every Sabbath until 2:00 p.m. They would have to book weddings after that hour.

I sold my home in Denver and moved up to my nearly 1,200 square-foot condo. The Summit Fellowship of Seventh-day Adventist Church had its beginnings near here over twenty years ago.

This is God's church, and we are His servants. Over the years, we have been so blessed to welcome people from all over the world, whether they be skiers/snowboarders in the wintertime, or hikers, bikers, backpackers, campers, or mountain climbers in the summertime.

I thank the Lord that in spite of me, He has blessed our church family. I wish I had time to share some of the testimonies of those who have attended our church through these years, who often have come from a background of drugs, alcohol, abuse, and other issues, to go on to become pastors, evangelists, and true followers of the Lord.

I do want to mention one specific blessing. Some dear friends by the names of Carol Chanslor, and Dr. Keith and Sherrie Mack, came to visit our church after they had seen me on 3ABN (once again giving my abbreviated testimony).

They wanted to live up here, but due to the altitude, were not able to handle the lack of oxygen. Carol, however, donated both a beautiful grand piano and an organ, which have proven to be wonderful gifts ever since.

If you are ever in the mountains of Colorado, please make it a point to stop in and worship with us. Look us up at Copper Mountain Chapel, 630 Copper Road, Copper Mountain, Colorado.

Turning Over a Whole New Leaf

Shortly after the Cordminder fiasco, I decided to get back into the men's sportswear business helping to liquidate private label high-end merchandise.

When I had been studying the Bible with the associate pastor, he mentioned that he thought there were Adventists who lived around the corner from my place.

Sure enough, Dr. and Mrs. Robert Horner became not only dear friends, but also helped me stay close to the Lord. They would pick me up and take me to church, then bring me over to their home for lunch.

Following my accident, they were always there to help and encourage me. One day when I was having a pity party, they announced that they were going to take me on a Maranatha project. Up to that point, my idea of roughing it was not being able to call for room service!

We ended up in Santo Domingo for three weeks. After the first three days, I insisted that I had to go home. I wish I had time to tell you the story, but I can assure you the experience was a total culture shock to my system.

Next, the Horners took me to an ASI (Adventist-laymen's Services & Industries) national convention, which was the best experience of my life. I never missed a convention from that time on. I realized that my walk with the Lord was not where it should be and devoted my life to working with ASI.

Next, we ended up at the It Is Written Partnership meetings, which continued to be a blessing in my life. I loved all the ministries that were affiliated with ASI.

After attending one of the ASI national conventions, I discovered that there were over 151 witnessing tools that various ministries had developed to win souls to God's kingdom. I even wrote a booklet titled *Witnessing Made Simple*. Unfortunately, it is out of date now, but if you ever want to be involved in ministry for the Lord, go to an ASI convention and see all the many wonderful ways to share Christ. I promise you that it will be the best experience of your life.

In time, I was privileged to serve on the national ASI board as both the VP of finance and VP of membership, as well as serving four times as president of our ASI Mid-America regional chapter.

ASI developed a collection of evangelism resources titled New Beginnings, teaching laypeople how to set up small-group home Bible studies using the New Beginnings training materials developed by Mark Finley and a group of ASI members.

My friend Leasa and I would travel all over Inter-America, South America, Europe, the Philippines, and other countries, training thousands of laypeople how to share Christ. Later, I would go with various other people or alone and conduct training mostly in all the countries of South America, as well as Canada and Paris, France.

Part of my training would involve sharing my testimony as to how the Holy Spirit and the power of prayer brought me into the remnant church. In doing so, I would brush over my childhood upbringing, as I didn't want to have to deal with it. Most of the people simply assumed that I had not had any experience with Seventh-day Adventist teachings until remembering the little song, "Jesus Loves Me." Rather than going into all the dysfunction of my childhood and early teens, I would just go right on sharing my testimony.

Now for the last confession that my prideful heart must unburden. When I was twelve years old, I went to live with my two aunts, as I mentioned earlier. They both worked long hours as nurses, and the older one worked as a licensed practical nurse with private patients for twenty hours at a time.

My younger aunt was a head nurse at a large hospital in Evanston, Illinois. She was the one who had been molested by her brother between the ages of eight and eleven. Due to that trauma and despite being a member of the Mensa society for her high IQ, she later became bipolar and was hospitalized three times.

While I was living there, the older aunt molested me shortly after I had gotten dressed for bed. I won't go into all the details, but it was very traumatic.

One evening while we were eating dinner, I must have objected to having to eat a certain food. Out of the blue, that aunt struck me across the face and told me to eat it or go straight to bed.

I began to cry. When I stood up, she grabbed me by the arm and told me something that would forever shape my life. "You know that your mother is a *Jew*, don't you?"

I had no idea what that meant and just pretended that I knew. It came out sounding like something that must be the worst possible disease anyone could possibly have.

From that day on, I buried my ancestral heritage and lied whenever anyone asked about my mother's nationality. You see, even now, when some of my friends will read this, they might make some comment such as, "That is why she must be such a good businesswoman," while down deep they still bear prejudice regarding Jews.

I can't tell you how this sin has haunted me for so many years, even since I became an Adventist.

If I asked the Lord to forgive me a million times, it would not compare to the nights I would lie awake and plead with the Lord to help me confess all my sins, especially those vague, distant ones.

I so desperately wanted approval from people. The little child in me thought, *If I could just be perfect enough, then I would be loved.*

I was so worried about what others thought of me that I was willing to forsake complete honesty for a short time, thinking that I might be okay.

Many nights and days, a disturbing thought kept going through my mind: You can't con God. Do you want to miss out on eternity in exchange for the approval of your friends and acquaintances?

You see, all the dysfunction in my childhood and yes, my adulthood, come down to whether I was willing to face the issues in my life and not only be honest with my friends and acquaintances, but most importantly with the Lord. I can pretend that I am just fine on the outside, but when all the layers are peeled away, I am empty without Jesus, my Redeemer and my Friend.

No matter what our sins may have been, we can't let pride cover them up. I spent so many years trying to be something I wasn't, so that my friends would think I was "okay" for them to like.

Just a thought: Could it be that Jesus will retain His Jewishness in Heaven?

No matter what people may say, there is still a stigma attached to being a Jew. I think that Jesus must have known this was going to be the case. Maybe that is why he came to Earth at the very time He chose. He knew ahead of time that to many people being a Jew would always involve a stigma.

All Christians are a part of the heritage of Israel and thus called the children of God, but so many times, people just bury that fact and think, *We're not Jews, and only Gentile Christians will be counted worthy in God's kingdom.*

I am Blessed, happy and pleased to be both a Jew and a Gentile who has been graphed in to the stock of Israel.

Whatever your own personal religious persuasion may be, I humbly ask your forgiveness in not telling you the complete story of who I truly am and what my childhood was like, that is, until now.

The most important thing to me is to be in God's kingdom along with all of those who have been a part of my life. I pray that now that I have confessed my past, those who truly are my friends will remain so. For those who cannot continue as my friends, I pray for you.

The little child in me who pleads for approval from people now pleads only for approval from the Lord who loves me and who gave His life to save me.

I had to make a choice eventually: either con my family, friends, and acquaintances, or con God. Believe me, I have found out a very important fact the hard way: YOU CAN'T CON GOD.

Women's News

26-YEAR-OLD DISCOVERS PLACE FOR FEMININITY

Hotel Executive Finds Ro

at Top

Barbara Taylor is motivated to succeed

Features

She's Boss in Playboy's Man's World

Barbara Effects Reversal Of Playboy Club Fortunes

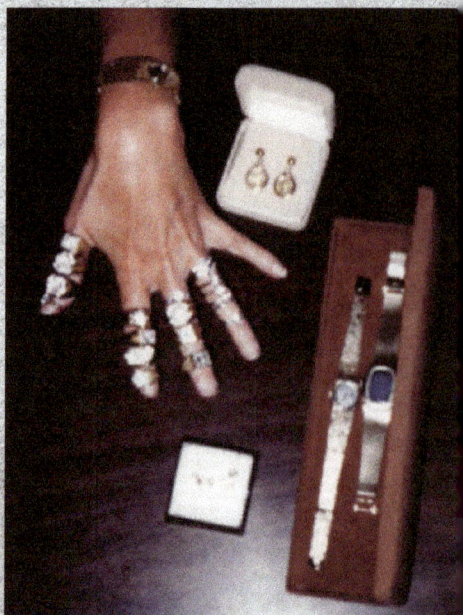

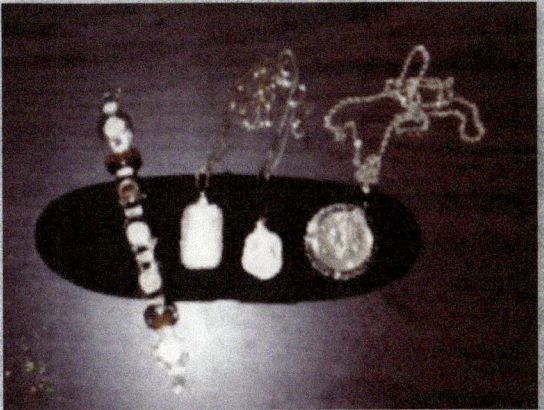

Barbara Taylor in her showroom at the Denver Mart.

BUSINESS

SOUTH **DENVER** METRO

CORPORATE
CONNECTION
A Smith Publication

Vol. 4, No. 4

Retail Begins Bounce

**The Hidden Society/
The Homeless**

90s Women to Watch

FEATURE

Women to Watch

CORPORATE CONNECTION MAGAZINE
selects six outstanding women for 90s.

By Nina Bondarook

Success. To many, it's as elusive as the Fountain of Youth. Some say it's the result of hard work and goal-setting, and others still are trying to achieve it. South Metro Denver is teeming with women worth watching in all professions. **CORPORATE CONNECTION MAGAZINE** is proud to feature six women representing different facets of business: entrepreneurs, women who began their career, or second career, later in life, and others whose goal is to help younger women succeed.

Sixty-five-year old **Ann Sink White** of Cherry Creek is a graduate of Bennington College, Bennington, Vermont. While has spent her lifetime acquainting friends, neighbors and the children she taught in Littleton and Cherry Creek Schools, to appreciate art. An accomplished artist herself, White was a founding member, in 1963, of a group of distinguished Colorado Artists who started "The Nine." The Nine were friends who displayed their work in each others' homes in order to share collections and generate interest in the art world. Today, the group has expanded and produces an annual two-day show at Kent Country Day School in October.

White also is a member of the Alliance for Contemporary Art, which provides support to young artists, and is very involved with the Denver Art Museum as well as semi-retired. As for her secret to success: "I think you've got to be decorative, for a while, of

Ann Sink White

Barbara Taylor

people you like and respect. Then, develop your own style. Don't be afraid to experiment, try new things."

Barbara Taylor also believes in a good education. As co-founder and president of the Buck Corp. of Littleton, the only woman-owned communications company in America, Barbara Taylor's message is one of health education and safe sex. Buck markets "For Us" condoms nationwide and intends to become the front runner in open and factual discussions of sexually transmitted diseases. Taylor entered the $400 million condom industry two years ago, after successful careers in marketing for Pluribus International, and sells is part owner of Lord Jeff men's sportswear company, which has annual sales in excess of $45 million. She also has taught sales and marketing at the University of Colorado, and is a chemistry/pre-med major at the University of Denver.

Why condoms? "Today in the United

States, one in five people has a sexually transmitted disease. There are more than 40 sexually transmitted diseases, many of them life-threatening, and all are seen to mean about to ADDS. I want to help educate America's youth, so that they'll protect themselves.

Mindy Hartman-Rodwell's position as manager of finance operations, budgeting and planning for the National Division, East Group of American Television & Communications Corp. (ATC) of Englewood, underscores her success in the business world. But, her personal challenges associated with overcoming the complications of a car accident four years ago, and the ongoing frustrations of being confined to a wheelchair magnify her accomplishments.

Hartman-Rodwell, 39, received a BA in Business Administration 10 years ago from Colorado College, and started her ATC career as an employee of the budget and rate department. In the short

Mindy Hartman-Rodwell

Newsweek

January 16, 1978 / $1.00

How Men Are Changing

Reader's Digest

February 1978   95¢

Unforgettable Bing Crosby .... Bob Hope 65
Searching for Mankind's Roots .... Ronald Schiller 70
Soviet Civil Defense: The Grim Realities ... John G. Hubbell 17
Fourth Down, 30 Centimeters to Go

What You Do—And Do Not—Owe Your Children ... Kansas City Star Magazine 81

Niki Lauda's Duel With Death .... Ann Landers 85
My Father's Farm .... Drama in Real Life 88
New Light on Cholesterol .... Rolling Stone 94
A Valentine of Love Letters .... Stanley L. Englebardt 100
Operation Sting: How the Cops Conned the Crooks "Love Letters" 104
                                      "Surprise! Surprise!" 107
Questions Couples Ask Sex Therapists Most

Nightmare   Norman M. Lobsenz 115
Riding the

A Small Mic

Masterpiece
Consumer "

The Trouble
Jaguar in th
ESDs—Thos
The Town T

Return to C

Book! T
Section I

The Other M
Power, 21—
Quotes, 48—
of Medicine,
71—Points t
Best Medicine

37th year: O

People weekly

December 26–January 2, 1978 · $1

SPECIAL DOUBLE ISSUE

the 25 most intriguing people of 1977

& The faces to watch in 1978

The Barlo approach:
protection from a woman's point of view.

Now and into the 90s, women must take responsibility for their own protection from sexually transmitted diseases. AIDS, chlamydia, gonorrhea, herpes and other sexually transmitted diseases have their own critical consequences. No woman can afford to rely on someone else to take care of her health. That's why 70% of all condoms are currently purchased by women . . .and why two astute businesswomen are challenging the giants of the industry by marketing condom products which are superior in strength yet don't distort sensation. FOR-US™ products offer a better alternative, and the peace of mind every customer seeks. The female of the 90s is looking for a product designed with her in mind.

FOR-US is that product!

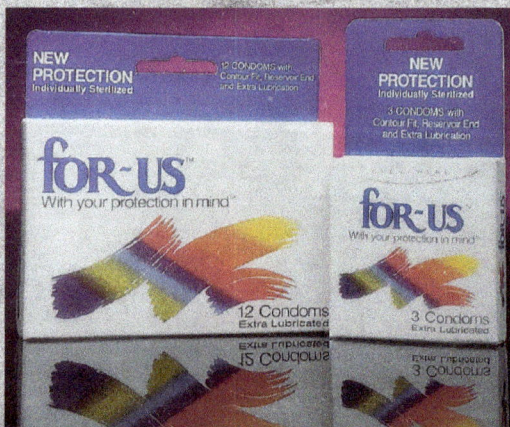

Accident challenges entrepreneur

AFTERWORD

He that worketh deceit shall not dwell within My house: He that telleth lies shall not tarry in My sight. (Psalm 101:7)

For God shall bring every work into judgment, with every secret thing, whether it be good, or whether it be evil. (Ecclesiastes 12:14)

Resources

Adventist-laymen's Services & Industries (ASI) is an organization of Laymen/Laywomen, along with self-supporting ministries, whose motto is "Sharing Christ in the Marketplace." They help build schools, orphanages, hospital clinics, and aid in disaster relief programs both here at home and around the world, just to mention a few of their hundreds of ministries. Their funding goes 100% to each project. For more information go to: asiministries.org.

If you, like me, have gone through trauma in your life, I encourage you to get help. Jennifer Jill Schwirzer is an excellent counselor.

For those in search of biblically-grounded, scientifically-informed, wholistic, compassionate, counseling and coaching, go to Abide Network at www.abidecounseling.us/ and fill out the intake form. Abide also offers group workshops, Bible studies, and free telephone support groups.

About the Author

Barbara Elizabeth Taylor currently lives in Copper Mountain, Colorado. She travels extensively, training people on how to give Small Group Home Bible Studies. She has spent most of her adult life in achieving outstanding sales and marketing awards in various corporations and businesses. She loves spending time in the mountains and traveling around the world.

Her only prayer is that each and every one of you will totally surrender your heart to the Lord and accept the free gift of eternal salvation. We will only have one of two choices to make – eternal life or eternal death. Life is too short to choose the second.

Barbara Elizabeth Taylor is happy to share the New Beginning program with any of your churches that want to motivate people on setting up Small Group Home Bible Studies. She has been a motivational speaker throughout her career to corporations, as well as conferences and churches around the world and here at home.

The author can be contacted at between2@aol.com.

www.ingramcontent.com/pod-product-compliance
Lightning Source LLC
La Vergne TN
LVHW021121080426
835509LV00011B/1374